What If

Other books by Hydee Tehana

Fire and Water: Awakening the Dragon Within

What If…Death is a Doorway?

What If...

Belief Systems Are Just BS?

by

Hydee Tehana

Trinity Rose Productions, LLC
Kealakekua, Hawaii

What If...

Belief Systems Are Just BS?

Copyright © 2020 Hydee Tehana

All rights reserved. No part of this book may be used or reproduced by any means, graphic, electronic, or mechanical, including photocopying, recording, taping or by any information storage retrieval system without the written permission of the publisher except in the case of brief quotations embodied in critical articles and reviews.

Hydee Tehana's books may be
ordered through booksellers or Amazon.com.

What If...Belief Systems Are Just BS? is book two in the series of *What If* books.

Trinity Rose Productions, LLC
PO Box 1041
Kealakekua, HI 96750 USA

HydeeTehana.com
Hhtehana888@protonmail.com
ISBN: 978-1-7341995-3-6 (pbk)
ISBN: 978-1-7341995-8-1 (eBook)
ISBN: 978-1-7341995-5-0 (hbk)

Front cover image by Lisa Denning
http://lisadenning.com/

This book is dedicated
to Source and the evolution of humankind.

May we all awaken to the bigger picture and remember…

*"The important thing is not to stop questioning.
Curiosity has its own reason for existing."*
                    ~Albert Einstein

Foreword…

I've always enjoyed simple books that say so much with so few words. Our language is quite limiting and the energy behind the words or the essence "say" so much more with feeling. Being simple-minded and a kid at heart, I love simplicity with wisdom and clarity as I often feel we make things much more complicated than they need to be in this world.

This book is my vision of co-creating a simple-minded book with Source that explores what makes up beliefs and belief systems. Beliefs are truly fascinating and what we believe creates our reality around us. They can expand or limit our lives immensely. Unfortunately, beliefs often cause division and separation throughout our society.

Most of us don't even realize that we have them or how we "got" them as it starts very early in our lives! Our mind attaches itself to beliefs which are limited and seek solutions outside of ourselves. All answers are found by going within and listening.

People need something to believe in, yet believing is different than knowing. Knowing is from experience or from a deep "inner knowing." A journey into "the self" is where we become "real" or "realized," hence, "*Know Thyself*" as the saying goes. I have found as we shift perspectives, there are no absolute truths for there are many truths depending on the perspective you look at it from!

This book would not have happened had I not quieted my mind and listened. May you enjoy and feel into the essence of what resonates with your own beliefs and inner truth!

Are you ready to be curious and wonder why you believe what you do?

Ever wonder if your beliefs serve you or keep you stuck?

Are you ready for your life to be playful and magical again?

If so, let's dive in!

What is a belief?

Where do belief systems come from?

Are we born with them?

Does society, parents, schools, etc…play a part in forming our beliefs?

What do you think?

What is the definition of a belief?

The dictionary says that a belief is an acceptance that a statement is true or that something exists.

What is the definition of a system?

The dictionary says that a system is a group of related parts that move or work together.

So, a belief is something you came to accept that is true and the system is how that belief works together in this reality.

Now, let's look at some beliefs and how they got there…

Let's take an example of looking at part of the name of this book.

What did you think about seeing BS?

Bull Shit? Or Belief Systems?

Let's go one step further…

Do you believe that the word "shit" is a "bad" word?

If so, where did this belief come from?

If you research where the word "Shit" came from, you would find that it was an abbreviation used when shipping cow manure years ago on boats.

They wrote on it, "Ship High In Transport" which became abbreviated as S.H.I.T.

Still a "bad" word?
Who made it a "bad" word?
Why are some words "bad" anyways?

Having fun yet?
Let's explore some other beliefs…

Belief Systems Are Just BS?

Is it your belief that dogs are kind and loving?

Or is it your belief that dogs are mean, scary, and not to be trusted?

Ever wonder how you came to believe that?

Can you change your beliefs?

Perhaps, if you decide you can.

There is no right or wrong about your belief, but only your belief that guides you in how to answer.

What's true for you?

Is it based on your experience?
Is it based on what others have experienced?

Did you blindly accept someone else's belief?

My Grandmother died of cancer.

Is it my belief that I will get cancer and die because she did?

Maybe?
Maybe not?

Do I have a choice?

If I believe that I will because she did, will I get cancer?

Will my belief "turn on" my genes to get cancer?

Vegetables are good for me.

Processed foods are not.

Is this my belief?

Is this true?

What if I believe the opposite is true?

What if I like to eat hamburgers every day?

What if I like to smoke cigarettes every day?

What if I eat hamburgers and smoke cigarettes every day and live to be 100 years old?

Do I really have this much power?

Perhaps we need to do experiments and testing to see if this is true?

What does the person doing the experiment believe?

Will this influence the outcome?

So many questions!

Is your head spinning yet?!

I was told all my life that I can do and be whatever I wanted.

I believed this.

What if I didn't?

Belief Systems Are Just BS?

I was told all my life that I was stupid and would never amount to anything.

I believed this.

What if this isn't true?

What if I didn't believe this?

What If

I was born blind and told that I would never drive a car or be able to read.

I read and drive a car today.

How can this happen?

I didn't believe what I was told.

I knew I would see.

I believed it and my eyes got better.

I was determined.

How can this happen?

Humans are born peaceful, kind, and loving.

Do you believe this?

Perhaps you believe that there will be peace on Earth?

Belief Systems Are Just BS?

Humans are cruel, evil, and born with sin.

Do you believe this?

Perhaps you see humanity as cruel and evil?

Is this true?

Ever really looked deeply into the eyes of a newborn baby?

What we believe, we make REAL in our reality.

Is it all just perception?

What are you creating?

Are you just reacting to your misdirected thoughts?

Are we not the creative mind of Source?

Is this statement just a belief?

How does experience shift beliefs?

What if we truly are the creative mind of Source?

What if we are made up of Source (God) stuff?

Does this challenge your beliefs?

What If

What if what we believe, we make REAL in our reality?

If we believe the world is dangerous, then it is, and we see danger everywhere.

If we believe the world is safe, then it is, and we experience safety everywhere.

What if a person comes to a computer and says, "These things never work for me. I always have issues with them."

Guess what?

Then, the person always has issues with computers and they don't work for them.

Did their belief just influence their reality?

Are we really that powerful?

What if a person says, "I love computers and they work great for me."

Guess what?

Everything goes smooth and the computer works great.

Why is that?

Is it listening to us?

Is the universe listening to us?!

It's all about energy…

and the intent we put into it.

Everything is conscious and listening.

Everything.

Our bodies are 70-80% water.
Water carries whatever energy is put into it.
It doesn't judge.

It's the intent of the energy or the belief that limits or frees.

Yep.

It's really that simple.

Does this make you want to control your thoughts, yet?

Can we actually control our thoughts?

Are we doomed to a "busy" mind with many thoughts?

What if our minds are so powerful that our thoughts are creating our world just by the thoughts we think?

Does it make you want to watch what thoughts you have that you put out into this world?

Can we direct our thoughts?

Of course, we can!

Ever heard of the movie, *Men Who Stare at Goats*?

We are incredibly powerful.

Are you creating consciously or unknowingly?

I once knew a captain in the fire department who said, "We always get an emergency call at two in the morning."

Guess what?!

He always did get a call around 2 am!

Did he create his reality?

Are we REALLY this powerful?

YES!

Yes, **YOU** are!

Belief Systems Are Just BS?

Does feeling that last statement make you excited or does that bring fear up in you?

It's okay either way…just notice it.
And then be curious about it.

Breathe.
And breathe again.

Pay attention to what happens next.

What If

What if the world is your blank canvas and you can create anything?

What would you create?

What if you are "God" disguised as a human?

What if we are all creator beings?

Did you choose this life?

What if you are not a victim?

Are you happy with what you have created around you in your life?

What if you had a magic wand and you said, "Abracadabra!"

This means to create what you speak.

Have we forgotten?
We are magical!

Words have energy within them and create with your intention.

Are you cursing and sending spells with your words or creating beauty around you?

It's your choice!
Remember?!

What If

We are powerful as individuals.
We are even more powerful as a group.

Is this true?

Ever wondered how a rain dance worked?

Focused intention of a group is incredibly powerful and it multiplies.

And who knows…

Perhaps this is how our ancestors moved large stones at places like Stonehenge?

Belief Systems Are Just BS?

Come up with an intention.

Believe it.
Truly believe it.

Vision it from your heart space.
Know it will be and let go of the outcome.

Watch what happens!

What If

Don't see what you asked for yet?

Remember, this is a denser reality system and it takes some "time" to see it.

Or does it?

Keep believing.
It's already happening.

Get in your heart space and it will manifest instantly!

Make sure you truly believe what you are asking for.

Because your subconscious mind may be saying and believing something else.

What are the programs running in the background of your mind?

How did they get there?
Do they affect your thoughts and actions?

They sure do!

What is the subconscious mind?

Are you aware of the voice in your head?

Can you hear it?
We all have it.

No, you are not schizophrenic.
This is just a label to make us feel that we are disconnected.

Belief Systems Are Just BS?

Our subconscious holds all types of beliefs especially from when we were little kids.

Do you ever hear your mother's or father's voice speaking?

"You are amazing."
"You are not good enough."
"You did a good job!"
"You are stupid."
"You are blah, blah, blah…"

Why are you listening to "those" voices instead of your own inner voice?!

It's all just a program…our subconscious.
It keeps running in the background of our lives.

It was programmed what to believe when we were kids.

Do you remember or perhaps you don't?
Perhaps it's part of you and you don't know any different?

Do you know the "still" part of yourself or just the part that thinks you are this human body?

Belief Systems Are Just BS?

Honestly, no judgment here.

Our parents had the same thing done to them, and their parents to them, and on and on...

Are we destined to repeat this programming over and over?

Can you break this cycle?

Absolutely!

What will you choose?

Let's look at simple programming that usually happens when we are kids.

Take the example of learning to ride a bike.

When you first learn, you are paying attention to everything.

You pay attention to where your feet are, how to move your hands, balancing, etc...

Your consciousness is aware of everything.

Then, a few months later, you just pick up the bike and ride!

No thinking!
How does this happen?

Because it is now a program that your subconscious knows.

We really do very little thinking as most of our thinking is programmed.

The program plays over and over and over...

So, unless you are CONSCIOUS and paying attention to your thoughts, your subconscious will run you!

No judgment here.
Kinda wild to think about!?

The subconscious just plays programs…like a computer.

No need to judge if this is good or bad.

The subconscious is just doing what it is supposed to do…what it was programmed to do!

Perhaps we are just robots?
Maybe some of us are?
Or perhaps we are just zombies?

Is that why they call it TV **programming**?

Are we being programmed to someone else's beliefs when we watch television?

Perhaps.

"Tele" means transmitting over a distance.
"Vision" means the power of seeing.

Whose vision are you seeing and believing?

Belief Systems Are Just BS?

What about the belief that we need to eat breakfast in the morning because it is the most important meal of the day?

Who decided this?
How about this instead…

How about we eat when we are hungry because our body is telling us this?

What a novel idea, right?

Ever heard of people that were told by their doctor that they have cancer and have 6 months to live?

Then, they die at exactly 6 months or close to that.

Did they believe what their doctor told them? Were they a good student and listened to their teacher?!

Belief Systems Are Just BS?

Ever heard of a thirty-eight year old being told that they would die in two years from a fatal disease, yet they are still alive at seventy-four years of age?

Ever heard of Steven Hawking and his disease? His doctors told him he would die in two years when he was forty.

He didn't believe them.
Bad student?

What If

What really makes this world come together
with so many beliefs?

It is our participation in this reality system.
We chose to make it the way it is.
If we don't like it, let's create what we want.

Do we want a world that is life giving?
We can have that if we choose.

Do we want a world that is based on death and
destruction?

We can have that if we choose.

What do you want?

Belief Systems Are Just BS?

This may all sound like some new age BS, but ask yourself why you cherish your opinions?

Also known as…Beliefs.

How did you come to believe this?
How did I come to believe this?

Is this just a book about me spilling my BS?!

Perhaps.

What is truth anyways?

Perhaps our truths are colored by our experiences and then, we form our beliefs?

Or is this how we "know" things?

Does it matter how our beliefs got there or that we recognize them?

Are all religions just belief systems?
Do religions make us feel closer to spirit?
Are they designed to control humans?
Do they separate or unite us?
Are they designed to make us feel guilty or not worthy?

Are they used to make us attack each other?

"I am right, I believe…"
"You are wrong because you believe…"

Perhaps someone doesn't like a certain religion, so they make up their own. Ever wonder why Lutheran and Catholicism are so closely related?

Who came up with all these religions?

Ever question that?

Do they come from love or fear?

Do they make you feel good about yourself?

What's the difference between religion and spirituality anyways?

Why do placebos work as well as or better than medications without side effects?

Is it because of what the doctor tells you and how it will heal you?

Perhaps because of your beliefs in them?

Are beliefs that powerful!?

Again, are we just a bunch of robots from our programming?

Ever see the kid's movie, *The Lego Movie*?
Perhaps we are just programmed how to be?

Are we to not question anything?

Do we have a choice?
What do you believe?

So, how do you remove the programming?
How do you re-wire the subconscious mind?

Or are you screwed?!

No, you aren't.
Our brains can be reprogrammed.

Ever heard of neuroplasticity?
Our brains are amazing.

Let's look at a simple way to first acknowledge any programs that are running.

First, become totally aware and conscious of the voice in your head.

Then, be the conscious observer of that voice and watch the thoughts without judgment.

Just watch.
Be curious.
Let go of judgment.
Breathe.

You are not your thoughts.
Breathe and give it space.

Allow breath to be your guide.
Notice how certain thoughts make you feel.
Give more attention to the ones that feel good.

For the thoughts that feel bad, put your hand
over your heart and say out loud, "Thank you."

Then, move into the stargate of your heart as
you leave the old programs behind.

You simply "meld" into your heart space
following it through to where that program no
longer exists.

Now, think of something that makes you smile!
Focus on that and keep smiling!

Remove the "story" from the body energetically and dissolve all memories, wounds, and limiting beliefs that confirm our fear-based sense of separation.

It's that simple.
It's all about frequency.

It is possible or do you not believe it?
Or maybe you don't wanna let go of your story?

All good.
You don't have to.
Remember, it's your story.

You can decide how you want the story to be written.

Belief Systems Are Just BS?

So, you are walking down the street and someone calls you "stupid."

Do you become upset or do you laugh?
How do they know if you are stupid or not?!

Are they projecting their belief about themselves onto you?

Is it true that you are stupid?
What does your subconscious believe?

Shine a spotlight on your thoughts.
It doesn't matter how they got there.
Decide which ones you want to keep.

Which ones do you want to listen to?

Imagination is everything.
Imagine how you want your life to be.

By believing your thoughts, you create
everything around you.

You can begin to "tele-vision" how you want to
vision your own life!

Are you limiting yourself?
Are you really this powerful?
What do you believe?

Is this all just a bunch of BS?!

Beliefs create thoughts.
Thoughts create words.
Words create actions.
Actions become habits.

Simple.

Welcome to your life that you created.

As you go through re-wiring your subconscious, have patience.

It took years to get that way.
And remember, you are never alone.

Ask your spirit guides and helpers to release all your limiting beliefs and re-wire your subconscious.

Yes, you have lots of help. Just ask, as everything is listening.

Again, when you notice an old program or belief, put your hand over your heart and say out loud, "Thank you!"

Now, meld into your heart space and you will literally, shift dimensions.

The program has been deleted!
The frequency has been vaporized!

Get ready to fly and be free!
Are you ready?!

Why is there a war on our beliefs?

Why do people argue about what others believe?

Is this a way to control us and keep us in chaos?
Is it a way to keep us separate instead of uniting us?

United we are strong.

What is the real agenda here?

Is television influencing our beliefs?
Who is behind the screen anyways?

Why is the media owned by six corporations?

What do "they" have to gain by getting you to believe "their" vision?

Are you helping "them" create "their" world?
Are "they" stealing your consciousness?

Better yet…are you ALLOWING them to?

What you focus on gains power. Focus only on what you want!

Do commercials influence our beliefs?

Ever felt like you had to have something after watching a certain commercial?

Ever fall asleep watching television?
I know I have.

Could your subconscious mind still be programmed during this?

You bet it can.
It is all about frequency.

Whose ideas are you believing?

Belief Systems Are Just BS?

Do schools influence our beliefs?

Who decides what is taught in schools and why?

What do you think?

Why don't we question things more?

Are we just "spoon-fed" what to believe and blindly accept it?

Do you believe everything you are taught?

Or do you question the reality around you?

Take a deep breath.
Center yourself.

Pay attention to what is going on in your body.
Become the conscious observer of you.

Get out of your head as that is just intellect and not who you truly are.

Your head is there to monitor if you are safe or not.

Your head has a limited solution set, but your heart has unlimited options.

Now, get into your heart space.
Place your hand on your heart and breathe putting your attention here.

As you put your attention on your body, what do you notice?

Can you feel your body?
Your body is very alive.

There is no right or wrong…just notice what is happening inside you.

Your true essence is felt in the body.

Is your body tingling?
Does your body feel alive?
Do you feel the energy?

Perhaps you can't feel your body?

It's all okay…just notice what is happening for you in this moment.

Breathe.
Breathe deeply.

Breathe deeply into your belly and into all the cells of your body.

There are really only two emotions…

Love and Fear.

All anger, jealously, lack, sadness, impatience, etc…come from fear.

All happiness, joy, laughter, passion, etc…come from love.

What will you choose?

You do have a choice.

Feel into this…

If you are not in your power, you are in fear.

Are you ready to step into your power?

Belief Systems Are Just BS?

Perhaps we need to unlearn our beliefs?

A belief is just a thought you think over and over again.

Where did we get them?

Oh, that's right…

From our parents, family, schools, leaders, doctors, television, society, etc…

Blah, blah, blah…

Try this out…

Is this whole reality an illusion?

What do you think?
What do you feel?

Are we being told what to think and feel?

Ever see the movie, *Wag the Dog*?

How easy is it to get the masses to believe what you want them to?

Belief Systems Are Just BS?

We limit ourselves through our beliefs.

And we can be LIMITLESS through our beliefs.

What will you choose?

It is totally up to you.

Focus only on what you want for what you focus on, gains power!

What do you truly believe?

Perhaps beliefs are a type of mind control?

What you believe, you become.

Start questioning your beliefs and where they came from.

Belief Systems Are Just BS?

If we are truly in control of our beliefs, what would you believe?

Does that make you uncomfortable to think about?

Do you not like to think of how powerful you are?

Do you like being a victim?
Do you like to be told what to believe?

WHY?

Do you want to stand in your power, yet?

Perhaps it is our energy or our intent that we put into our beliefs that make them real?

Is it really that easy?

IS IT THAT SIMPLE?

Yep.

Are we not here on this planet to create and manifest all things possible?

Are we master creators?

Do you remember yet?

Are we really that powerful and our beliefs influence our reality?

Have you forgotten?

Are you tired of me asking you questions yet?!

Belief Systems Are Just BS?

So, pay attention to your thoughts and release any subconscious beliefs that no longer serve you.

If you so choose, of course.

Are you coming from your heart space?
Are you operating from a place of love or fear?

Pay attention to your thoughts and how they make you feel.

Follow the ones that make you feel good.
Your whole world will change when you do!

Remember, your thoughts and feelings are the seeds that feed and create your reality.

So, if you notice yourself going into negative thoughts (the default victim pattern), change them immediately!

No judgement.

Find the next best feeling thought…

Keep your vibration at the highest level possible by focusing on anything that makes you happy!

Belief Systems Are Just BS?

Look at what you believe and how you are emotionally invested in your belief system.

Does this serve you?

Know that it is not the belief system itself that is causing you pain and disharmony.

It is the emotions that you are attaching to the belief system.

Your trauma is being caused by being emotionally attached to beliefs that are handed down from others.

Become fully conscious by being in the present moment.

It all depends on the eye of the beholder and what perspective you look at it from.

Should we kill each other because we have different beliefs and perspectives?

Perhaps all of us are RIGHT?!

Is the only absolute truth the "I AM" (the Source of everything)?

Perhaps there are no absolute truths?

For as consciousness evolves, perception and beliefs change.

There are many perspectives to look at things from. Are you on top of the mountain or down in the valley?

As perception broadens, your perspective shifts.

Is your mind blown, yet?

What do you truly believe?

Do you want to create the reality that you want to live in?

You are in control of your beliefs and your perspectives.

Whatcha think?

Is this book just a bunch of BS?

Perhaps?!

"A belief is nothing more than a chronic pattern of thought, and you have the ability--if you try even a little bit--to begin a new pattern, to tell a new story, to achieve a different vibration, to change your point of attraction.

The *Law of Attraction* is responding to your vibration, and you can easily change your vibrational point of attraction by visualizing the lifestyle you desire and holding your attention upon those images until you begin to feel relief, which will indicate that a true vibrational shift has occurred."
　　~Abraham-Hicks

About the Author

Hydee Tehana is really just a big kid in an adult body who sometimes acts her age while exploring this amazing universe. Her favorite age to be is eight because eight reminds her of being playful and full of wonder. She remembers the greater meaning of life and what it was like on the other side while taking on a human incarnation this lifetime.

The author began to remember more about what "life" is really about when "life" began to not make sense anymore. Hydee had it "all" and began questioning everything she was taught as a little girl by her parents, teachers, and society. Remembering more every day and getting out of the "matrix" of old programming, beliefs, and limitations is now something she no longer chooses to experience as all of life is meant to be magical, fun, and free.

Hydee loves adventure and travel along with swimming in the ocean with her ocean friends as much as possible. Time travel and teleportation are close to her heart. She loves the fire elemental as well as all the elements as she has a deep connection with all of Mother Nature.

Hydee was a Captain/paramedic in the fire department for just over twenty years. She also has her master's degree in psychology and is a licensed psychotherapist. Hydee is currently working on evolving consciousness on this planet through speaking, authoring books, producing enlightened movies, and most importantly, expanding her own consciousness.

To contact Hydee Tehana:

Hydeetehana.com
hhtehana888@protonmail.com

Belief Systems Are Just BS?

Made in the USA
Columbia, SC
18 June 2022